Afef Mdhaffar

Embedded Machine Learning

Afef Mdhaffar

Embedded Machine Learning

ScienciaScripts

Imprint
Any brand names and product names mentioned in this book are subject to trademark, brand or patent protection and are trademarks or registered trademarks of their respective holders. The use of brand names, product names, common names, trade names, product descriptions etc. even without a particular marking in this work is in no way to be construed to mean that such names may be regarded as unrestricted in respect of trademark and brand protection legislation and could thus be used by anyone.

Cover image: www.ingimage.com

This book is a translation from the original published under ISBN 978-620-6-70663-2.

Publisher:
Sciencia Scripts
is a trademark of
Dodo Books Indian Ocean Ltd. and OmniScriptum S.R.L publishing group

120 High Road, East Finchley, London, N2 9ED, United Kingdom
Str. Armeneasca 28/1, office 1, Chisinau MD-2012, Republic of Moldova, Europe
Printed at: see last page
ISBN: 978-620-8-15865-1

Contents

Description of the Document

This book contains the course material and partial tutorials (i.e., Python implementations) for the "Embedded Automatic Learning" module, taught to students in the "Embedded Systems" master's programme at the Ecole Nationale d'lngenieurs de Sfax (ENIS), Tunisia.

This book thus represents a first step towards embedded deep learning. It presents techniques for optimising and compressing deep learning models. These techniques facilitate the efficient deployment of a high-performance, lightweight deep learning model on resource-limited devices such as smartphones and microcontrollers.

This document also explores a current knowledge transfer technique, namely knowledge distillation. This technique makes it possible to improve the performance of a lightweight deep learning model, while transferring to it the knowledge of a complex, high-performance deep learning model.

All these techniques are detailed in this book and illustrated by practical Python implementations, generally based on the use of the pytorch and tensorflow libraries.

This book consists of six chapters. The first chapter is an introduction to the topic of embedded machine learning. This introduction leads to two introductory chapters, which deal with the two pillars of embedded machine learning: (1) machine learning and (2) connected objects. Chapters 2 and 3 introduce these two key concepts. Chapter 4 focuses on optimization and compression techniques that can be applied to deep learning models, such as pruning and quantization. The fifth chapter focuses on the knowledge distillation technique. Finally, this book is closed by a conclusion and some bibliographical references which have been used for the elaboration of this document.

Chapter 1

Introduction Generate

1.1 Context

[The emergence of machine learning has marked a revolution in data analysis, knowledge extraction and complex decision making. Machine learning techniques are now used in many areas of real life, such as medicine, agriculture and the automotive [. These solutions generally require high-performance machines to be trained and deployed.

This development in machine learning has been coupled with [the emergence of connected objects. We now live in a connected world where the [internet of things has become the [internet of the century. Every day, these connected objects deliver a huge volume of data, including [information and useful knowledge. This knowledge can easily be extracted using learning techniques, such as deep learning and reinforcement learning. However, this data remains delicate as it gives a global and detailed view of the individuals and their assets under surveillance. For example, the data collected by connected medical sensors is generally quite sensitive. It is therefore not acceptable to send this data to third-party servers for processing by solutions based on machine learning techniques. It is therefore essential to find the necessary means of adapting the performance required by learning techniques to connected sensors, such as ['Edge'] equipment.

1.2 Motivation

Given that these connected sensors are lightweight devices that do not have the necessary performance to run learning techniques, the researchers worked on compressing and [optimising solutions based on

The aim of this project is to develop a new approach to machine learning and deep learning, so that deep learning techniques can be embedded in lightweight devices such as smartphones, Raspberry Pi and Arduino boards. Hence the birth of a new line of research called "Embedded Automatic Learning".

1.3 Purpose of this book

This book aims to detail the process of compression and optimisation of deep learning models. It details (i) compression techniques such as quantization and pruning, and (ii) knowledge transfer techniques such as knowledge distillation.

1.4 Structure of this document

The remainder of this document is divided into 5 chapters. The first two chapters introduce two key concepts related to embedded machine learning, namely machine learning and the Internet of Things. The fourth chapter details the compression and optimisation techniques that can be used to reduce the size of deep learning models. This chapter focuses on the quantization technique and the pruning technique. The fifth chapter explores the knowledge distillation technique. This technique is considered as an up-to-date technique in the field of knowledge transfer.

Chapter 2

Introduction to machine learning

2.1 Introduction

This chapter introduces the subject of machine learning. It begins with a definition and an overview of its history. Next, we detail the theoretical foundations of machine learning. We then list the fields of application of machine learning. This chapter closes with a conclusion.

2.2 Definition and background

This section gives a definition of machine learning and details its historical context.

2.2.1 Definition

Automatic learning, also known as machine learning, is an essential part of artificial intelligence. It enables useful knowledge to be extracted from the data used for learning. It is an approach based on

learning from data and experience to develop intelligent computer systems, without having to program them explicitly.

2.2.2 Historical background

The concept of machine learning is not new. Based on mathematics and statistics, the first ANN saw the light of day in 1943. Shortly afterwards, researchers began to use the term "artificial intelligence". And from then on, computer scientists put in place the various building blocks of artificial intelligence. However, these advances only became a reality after the emergence of high-performance machines and the availability of sufficient data for learning. Machine learning has become quite popular since the emergence of deep learning and the Internet of Things. The increase in the number of connected objects means that a large volume of data is generated every day. This data is used for learning and has consequently demonstrated the potential of artificial intelligence and machine learning techniques for analysing data and extracting relevant knowledge.

2.3 Theoretical foundations

Machine learning is based on fundamental theoretical principles which form the foundation of its operation. This section provides an overview of these basic concepts. First, we give an overview of the most common types of learning. Next, we explain the learning process and give an overview of some of the techniques used in machine learning. We then focus on the data and models that form the core of the machine learning model.

2.3.1 Types of learning

There are three main types of learning: (i) supervised learning, (ii) unsupervised learning and (iii) reinforcement learning. These types are described below.

— **Supervised learning** is based on the use of labelled data. The aim is to teach a model on a set of annotated data. In this way, a response known in advance is associated with each example of data. This allows the model to be learned from these labelled correspondences. This type of learning is similar to human learning, where a child learns to speak from his mother or a pupil learns from his teacher.

— Unlike supervised learning, **unsupervised learning** models are based on unlabelled data. In this way, this learning mode is designed to discover the different representations of the data, without knowing the answers in advance.

— **Reinforcement Learning** (RL) enables an agent to learn decisions (i.e. launch appropriate actions) based on its interactions with an environment, which defines the problem to be solved. Depending on the actions taken by the agent, it receives bonuses or penalties. This strategy enables the agent to learn to maximise its bonuses over time, thereby learning to take appropriate actions.

2.3.2 Machine learning techniques

Machine learning is based on a variety of techniques and approaches. This section gives an overview of the best-known machine learning approaches, namely neural networks, ensemble methods, decision trees and support vector algorithms (SVMs).

Neural networks are currently the most widely used approach, particularly as they form the basis of deep machine learning. The idea behind neural networks is inspired by the structure of the human brain. A neural network is made up of several interconnected layers. Each layer is made up of several neurons. This structure makes it possible to learn complex representations.

Ensemble methods involve combining the predictions of several models to improve system performance. There are various examples of ensemble methods, such as boosting, bootstrap aggregating, voting and stacking. Ensemble methods are outside the scope of this book and will therefore not be discussed in detail.

Support vector algorithms (SVMs) are generally used to solve classification and regression problems. In the case of a classification problem, the aim is to find a hyperplane that separates the different classes. In the case of a regression problem, SVM seeks a hyperplane that minimises the prediction error, while tolerating a certain epsilon of error, around the data points.

Decision trees are generally used to solve classification and decision-making problems. A tree is made up of nodes, branches and leaves. A node represents a decision based on a particular characteristic. A branch, which runs from one node to another, represents the different possible values of the characteristic under consideration. Finally, the leaves represent the final decisions. The major advantage of using decision trees lies in their interpretability. This structure makes it easy to interpret the results obtained.

In the remainder of this book, we will focus solely on neural networks.

2.3.3 The learning process

The learning process involves two main phases. Firstly, the data must be collected and prepared. Secondly, the model must be defined so that it can be learned from the data that has already been prepared. The success of the first stage is crucial to obtaining a properly learned model. In fact, the model's performance depends greatly on the training data. Data preparation consists mainly of cleaning up and transforming the data into a suitable format that can be considered as input to the model. The model is created to be trained on the pre-prepared data, while adjusting its hyper-parameters and trying to minimise the loss function. The hyper-parameters are parameters external to the model, which influence the learning process. However, their values cannot be learned from the training data. These parameters are defined before training begins and can be adjusted as the training progresses by the developer, to optimise the model's performance. Hyper-parameters can include factors such as epochs number, model architecture (i.e. number and nature of layers), learning rate, batch size and regularisation (n, L2).

The loss function measures the difference between the model's predictions and the ground truth labels. Our main aim is to minimise this loss function at the learning stage. This leads us to more realistic predictions.

2.3.4 Data and models

Machine learning is mainly based on data. Data plays a crucial role in model learning. A machine learning model can be seen as a mathematical/algorithmic representation learned from data. The data format can be varied. It is possible to process images, videos, audio sequences and time series. The volume and quality of the data inevitably has an impact on the performance of the models. In fact, a model is best learned on a fairly representative set of data, with a sufficient quantity, inducing a wide variety of cases. In this way, a machine learning model can solve several problems, such as image classification, prediction in time series and hotel recommendations. A model is the result of training a neural network, as shown in Figure 2.1.

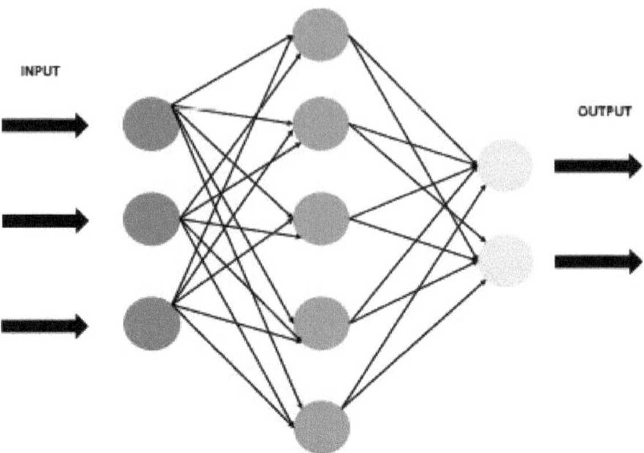

FIGURE 2.1 - Neural network

A neural network is generally characterised by a certain number of parameters which will be learned during the training phase. These parameters include:

— Weights: Each connection (i.e., illustrated by arrows in Figure 2.1) between neurons (i.e., illustrated by circles in Figure 2.1) in a model has an associated weight. These weights are learned and adjusted during the learning phase, allowing the model to correctly learn the relationships between the data, via mathematical representations.

— Biases: These are constant terms added to the weighted input of a neuron. They are learned during the training phase. The biases bring a certain reliability to the model by allowing it to move the activation function. The activation function introduces some non-linearity to the model, allowing it to learn complex patterns. Done, the role of the activation function is to decide whether to switch a neuron on or off. There are several activation functions, such as the sigmoid function, the ReLU function and the Softmax function.

— Activation function coefficients: Depending on the case, it is possible to choose an activation function from those listed. For example, if our model uses the ReLU activation function, then we need to specify a few parameters such as the slope coefficient for the ReLU.

— Normalization parameters: These parameters can include batch normalization parameters. These can be used to speed up learning and optimise model stability.

2.3.5 Evaluation methods and metrics

The devaluation of machine learning solutions is an essential step in the creation of reliable and effective models. This evaluation is generally carried out using various approaches. These approaches are listed below.

— The calculation and analysis of performance metrics such as Precision, Recall, Fi-measure, Confusion Matrix and ROC curves.

— Cross-validation as in K-fold cross validation

— Monitoring of the learning phase by displaying learning curves and loss function curves

— Statistical significance tests, such as the T-student test

It is always essential to compare the solution's performance against existing and competing solutions.

2.4 Applications

Machine learning has been applied in 'almost' every area of real life. For example, deep learning has been successfully used in the detection and prediction of epileptic seizures. Also, we notice the use of deep generative models like GAN (Generative Adversrial Network) and diffusion in the generation of medical data (e.g., ECG, EEG, ...etc). Also, reinforcement learning approaches have been used in (i) the selection of the best treatments in personalised medicine, (ii) trading and (iii) intelligent agriculture.

2.5 Conclusion

This chapter has introduced the subject of machine learning. It focused on its fundamental concepts and detailed the key information that will be essential for understanding and assimilating the following chapters.

Chapter 3

The emergence of connected objects

3.1 Introduction

The emergence of embedded machine learning is closely linked to the development of connected objects in the age of the Internet of Things (IoT). These objects generate a large volume of data every second, encouraging researchers to develop solutions based on learning and deep learning. However, these connected objects generally collect sensitive data which must be protected to ensure the privacy of their users. It is for this reason that embedded machine learning has emerged. Thus, it is still necessary to find techniques and approaches to be able to deploy these learning solutions on lightweight equipment, such as connected objects. This chapter provides an overview of (i) the Internet of Things: connected objects, underlying technologies and future developments, (ii) the integration of machine learning with connected objects and (iii) the challenges that arise from this.

3.2 Foundations of the Internet of Things

The Internet of Things is based on the use of intelligent interconnected objects. These connected objects are physical objects that have a processor, a storage system and a communication interface. Connected objects can be classified into two main categories, depending on the role they perform. We distinguish between sensors and actuators. Sensors are connected objects that capture and collect data. Actuators initiate actions.

3.2.1 Examples of connected objects

As Figure 3.1 illustrates, there are several connected objects around us. These include

FIGURE 3.1 - Connected objects

— Smartphones;
— Smartwatches such as Apple watch, Empatica Eд, Myo, Google watch and Withings ScanWatch;
— Connected medical sensors;
— Connected temperature sensors;
— Connected heart rate sensors;
— Connected agricultural sensors;
— Connected traps.

The Internet of Things is now virtually present in all areas of real life. The following section details the application areas of the Internet of Things.

3.2.2 Internet of Things applications

Today, we are seeing the presence of connected objects in various fields such as agriculture, medicine and smart cities. Different crops are currently being monitored using intelligent agricultural sensors. Actuators are also installed throughout the plots to take appropriate action. For example, olive plots are currently being monitored for intelligent and efficient irrigation. We are also seeing the emergence of connected traps for (1) detecting insects and pests and (2) spraying the right amount of insecticide. In the medical field, patients suffering from diabetes, cardiovascular disease and neurological disorders continue to be monitored. This monitoring makes it possible to analyse their state of health, detect (or even predict) crisis situations and take the necessary action.

3.2.3 Communication

Connected objects must be able to exchange data with each other efficiently. This exchange of data can be achieved using communication protocols such as MQTT or HTTP. These communication protocols allow devices to transmit information to other connected objects, gateways or cloud servers.

3.2.4 On-board systems

Connected objects must be able to run specific programs. This is ensured by the software embedded in the micro-controllers of these objects. Indeed, connected objects are generally equipped with micro-controllers such as Raspberry PI, arduino boards and ESPs. The embedded software must be designed to meet the time, space and energy constraints of lightweight equipment.

3.2.5 Security

It is essential to ensure the security of the data collected. For this reason, connected objects use encryption, authentication and access management mechanisms. Security standards such as TLS (Transport Layer Security) help to protect data. There are also IoT communication protocols that play an important role in data protection, such as the LoRaWAN communication protocol.

3.3 Integration of Machine Learning

The integration of machine learning into connected objects represents a major advance, enabling these devices to acquire more sophisticated capabilities. This section explores the fundamental role of machine learning in the context of connected objects, and the associated benefits and challenges.

3.3.1 Role of Machine Learning in Connected Objects

Machine learning enables intelligent analysis of the data collected by connected sensors. By integrating machine learning models into connected objects, they can make autonomous decisions based on the information they have learned. This enables real-time reactivity to changes in the environment, without the need for external intervention (i.e. by a third-party server). Also, the data remains on the connected objects since it y already processed. This protects the data and solves security-related problems.

3.3.2 Challenges of Embedded Machine Learning

[The integration of embedded machine learning is not a trivial task. In fact, it involves solving several challenges. These include hardware constraints. Connected objects are considered to be lightweight devices that are often limited in terms of computing power, memory and energy. On-board machine learning needs to be aligned with these constraints, using optimised algorithms and small-scale models. Energy efficiency and the ability to adapt to limited hardware resources are crucial challenges to overcome.

The aim of this book is to present techniques for optimising automatic learning models. The main focus is on compression techniques, such as quantization and pruning, and knowledge transfer techniques, such as knowledge distillation.

3.4 Conclusion

This chapter has detailed the foundations of the Internet of Things and demonstrated the importance of integrating machine learning into connected objects, while outlining the challenges that lie ahead. The next chapter is devoted to compression techniques for optimising deep learning algorithms.

Chapter 4

Compression techniques for deep learning models

4.1 Introduction

This chapter presents the compression techniques that could be used to optimise deep learning models. In this chapter, we discuss two main techniques, namely quantization and pruning.

4.2 Quantification

This section details quantisation and illustrates its use in the context of neural networks. We then present the main types of quantisation and discuss their advantages and disadvantages. This section details the quantization techniques. Each technique is illustrated by an example (i.e., python source code).

4.2.1 Generative definition of quantification

Quantization is a fairly robust compression technique that was originally used to compress images. It consists of representing image pixels on a reduced number of bits, while trying to maintain the same image quality. Figure 4.1 illustrates the quantisation process applied to the photo taken by the author of this book. This involves reducing the number of bits representing the pixels in the image. This will reduce the size of the image. As shown in figure 4.1, the number of bits can be reduced by

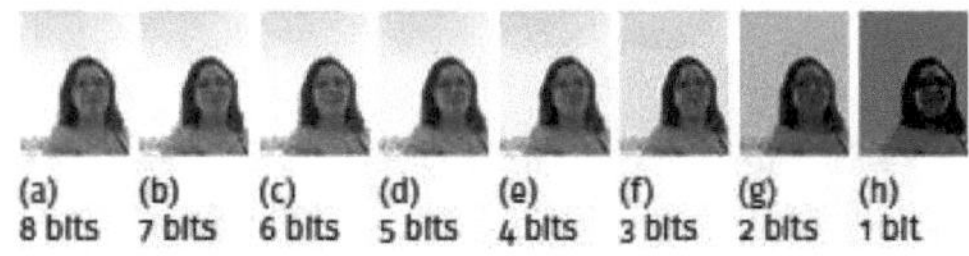

while maintaining the "same" image quality. But it is also possible for this step to result in a loss of image quality (see the representation of the same photo in a single bit).

Note that the Python source code used to quantify the photo in figure 4.1 is given in listing 4.1.

Listing 4.1 - Python code applied to obtain quantized images

```

from PIL import Image
import numpy as np

def quantize_image(image_path, output_path, num_bits):
    # Open the image
    img = Image.open(image_path)

    # Convert the image to a NumPy array
    img_array = np.array(img)

    # Quantize the image to the specified number of bits
    quantized_img = np.floor_divide(img_array, 256 // (2**num_bits))

    # Scale the values back to 0-255 range
    quantized_img = quantized_img * (256 // (2**num_bits))

    # Convert back to uint8 type
    quantized_img = quantized_img.astype(np.uint8)

    # Create a new image from the quantized array
    quantized_img = Image.fromarray(quantized_img)

    # Save the quantized image
    quantized_img.save(output_path)

# Example usage
```

```
image_path = 'afef.jpg'
output_path_template = 'output/quantized_image_{}.png'

bit_depths = [8, 7, 6, 5, 4, 3, 2, 1]

for bits in bit_depths:
    output_path = output_path_template.format(bits)
    quantize_image(image_path, output_path, bits)

print("Image quantization completed.")
```

4.2.2 Quantification and neural networks

The idea is to apply this principle of image quantification to the weights/activations of deep learning models. As да the weights/activations will be represented on a minimal number of bits. Admittedly, this reduction will affect the accuracy of the deep learning models but will make it possible to reduce their size considerably. This leads us towards the deployment of deep learning models on lightweight equipment.

There are two main types of quantification for deep learning models: (i) weight quantification and (ii) activation quantification.

4.2.3 Types of quantification

This section describes the types of quantisation.

4.2.3.1 Weight quantification

Quantifying the weights in deep learning models involves reducing the precision of the weight values. Weight values are generally represented in 32-bit floating point format. Quantisation involves reducing the binary representation of weight values to more compact formats such as integers or 16- or 8-bit floating points. This will reduce memory consumption, computing performance and energy consumption, while maintaining acceptable model performance.

4.2.3.2 Quantification of activations

As with weights, activations (i.e. outputs from neurons in a given layer) can also be quantified. This type of quantification depends largely on the activation function used. The activations represent the values calculated by the activation functions (e.g., Sigmoid, ReLU) in each layer of the network. These values can therefore be quantified in the same way as the weights. The aim of quantifying activations is to reduce the size of the values generated during inference. This will reduce the size of the activation values circulating through the network, thereby reducing the resources required for computation and storage.

4.2.4 Advantages and disadvantages of quantification

As already mentioned, quantization is a compression technique used mainly for image compression. It has been adopted to reduce the size of deep machine learning models, allowing them to be easily deployed on lightweight hardware. Quantization consists of reducing the number of bits representing the weight and activation values. This approach has both advantages and disadvantages. The advantages of weight quantization are:

— Reduction in the size of learning models, enabling more efficient deployment on lightweight equipment with limited memory resources.

— Reduced computing power requirements, accelerating inference on lightweight equipment such as smart sensors (i.e., connected objects) and mobile devices (i.e., smartphones).

— Narrowing the gap between learning models and real-time applications.

— Reduction in the amount of data transferred between the different layers of the neural network, in the case of quantification of activations.

— Speed of inference, in the case of quantification of activations.

The disadvantages of weight quantization are as follows:

— Possible reduction in accuracy, resulting in a loss of model performance.

— Strong dependency on the characteristics of the training data. Quantification results differ according to the nature of the training data.

— Managing the quantification of activations is more delicate than managing the quantification of weights. This is because some activation functions, such as the ReLU function, are sensitive to quantification. Implementing quantization of activations is therefore complex.

4.2.5 Quantification techniques

There are several quantification techniques which can be classified according to two main criteria: (i) the type of data (i.e., weights, activations) resulting from the quantification and (ii) the time of application of the quantification.

According to the first criterion (i.e., the type of data resulting from quantification), we discuss three main quantification techniques in this book:

— Full quantification

— Floating point quantification

— Binary and ternary quantification

According to the second criterion (i.e., the time at which the quantification is applied), we distinguish between two main quantification techniques:

— Quantification after training

— Quantification during training

4.2.5.1 Full quantification

This type of quantification allows weights/activations to be represented as integers rather than real numbers (i.e. floating point values). This significantly reduces the size of the models and speeds up inference. However, full quantisation results in a considerable loss of accuracy. Listing 4.2 illustrates the integer quantisation process using a simple example.

Listing 4.2 - Entire quantification

```
import torch
import torch.nn as nn
import numpy as np

# Définition d'un modèle simple pour l'exemple
class SimpleLinearModel(nn.Module):
    def __init__(self):
        super(SimpleLinearModel, self).__init__()
        self.linear = nn.Linear(10, 2)  # Une seule couche linéaire

    def forward(self, x):
        return self.linear(x)

# Fonction pour quantifier un tensor
def quantize_tensor(x, num_bits=8):
    qmin = 0  # Minimum de la plage de quantification
    qmax = 2**num_bits - 1  # Maximum de la plage de quantification
    min_val, max_val = x.min(), x.max()  # Valeurs min et max du tensor

    # Calcul de l'échelle et du point zéro pour la quantification
    scale = (max_val - min_val) / (qmax - qmin)
    zero_point = qmin - min_val / scale

    # Application de la quantification
    q_x = zero_point + x / scale
    q_x.clamp_(qmin, qmax).round_()  # Clamping et arrondissement
    q_x = q_x.round().byte()  # Conversion en byte (entier 8 bits)
    return q_x, scale, zero_point

# Fonction pour déquantifier un tensor
def dequantize_tensor(q_x, scale, zero_point):
    # Retour aux valeurs flottantes en utilisant l'échelle et le point zéro
    return scale * (q_x.float() - zero_point)

# Quantification des poids d'un modèle
def quantize_weights(model, num_bits=8):
    quantized_model_state = {}  # Dictionnaire pour les poids quantifiés
    scales = {}  # Dictionnaire pour les échelles de quantification
    zero_points = {}  # Dictionnaire pour les points zéro
    for name, param in model.state_dict().items():
        if 'weight' in name:  # Focus sur les poids
            q_param, scale, zero_point = quantize_tensor(param, num_bits)
            quantized_model_state[name] = q_param
            scales[name] = scale
            zero_points[name] = zero_point
    return quantized_model_state, scales, zero_points

# Déquantification des poids d'un modèle
def dequantize_weights(quantized_model_state, scales, zero_points):
    dequantized_model_state = {}  # Dictionnaire pour les poids déquantifiés
```

```
    for name, q_param in quantized_model_state.items():
        scale = scales[name]
        zero_point = zero_points[name]
        dequantized_model_state[name] = dequantize_tensor(q_param,
           scale, zero_point)
    return dequantized_model_state

# Exemple d'utilisation
model = SimpleLinearModel()
print("Poids avant quantification:", model.linear.weight)

# Application de la quantification
quantized_model_state, scales, zero_points = quantize_weights(model)
print("\nPoids quantifiés (affichage simplifié):",
   quantized_model_state['linear.weight'])

# Application de la déquantification
dequantized_model_state = dequantize_weights(quantized_model_state,
   scales, zero_points)
print("\nPoids après déquantification:",
   dequantized_model_state['linear.weight'])
```

The code in Listing 4.2 begins by defining a model containing a single linear layer (SimpleLinearModel). The aim of this example is to apply integer quantization to the weights of this model. Next, this example defines the "quan- tize_tensor" function. This function converts the floating-point values of a tensor into 8-bit integer values, while calculating a scale and a zero point. The values found are then used to approximate the original float values in quantized space. Our example then implements the 'dequantize_tensor' routine, which converts the quantized integer values to float values, using the scale and zero point calculated during quantization. This allows us to recover an approximation of the original float values in order to evaluate our results. Our code then quantises the model weights using the "quantize_weights" routine, which runs through all the model weights, quantises them using quantize_tensor, and stores the results along with the scaling and zero points. Finally, our code dequantizes the quantized weights using the dequantize_weights routine. The de-quantization step allows us to check the loss of precision caused by quantization. Figure 4.2 shows the weight values before and after quantisation.

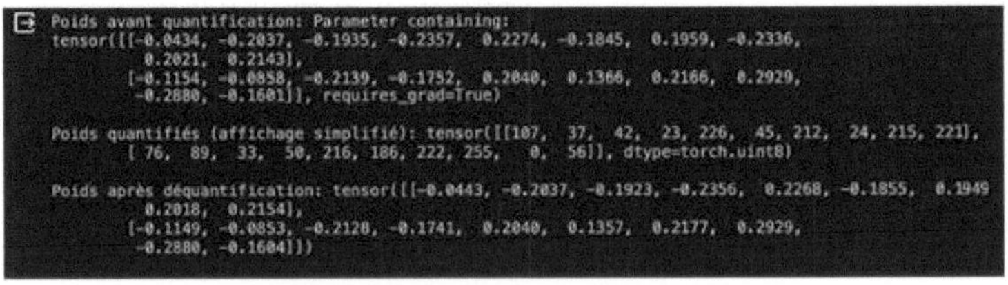

```
Poids avant quantification: Parameter containing:
tensor([[-0.0434, -0.2037, -0.1935, -0.2357,  0.2274, -0.1845,  0.1959, -0.2336,
          0.2021,  0.2143],
        [-0.1154, -0.0858, -0.2139, -0.1752,  0.2040,  0.1366,  0.2166,  0.2929,
         -0.2880, -0.1601]], requires_grad=True)

Poids quantifiés (affichage simplifié): tensor([[107,  37,  42,  23, 226,  45, 212,  24, 215, 221],
        [ 76,  89,  33,  50, 216, 186, 222, 255,   0,  56]], dtype=torch.uint8)

Poids après déquantification: tensor([[-0.0443, -0.2037, -0.1923, -0.2356,  0.2268, -0.1855,  0.1949
          0.2018,  0.2154],
        [-0.1149, -0.0853, -0.2128, -0.1741,  0.2040,  0.1357,  0.2177,  0.2929,
         -0.2880, -0.1604]])
```

FIGURE 4.2 - Before and after full quantification

4.2.5.2 Floating point quantification

This type of quantisation reduces the floating point representation of weights/activations by using shorter floating point formats (e.g. 8-bit floating points). This method is better than the previous method in that it allows a certain precision to be maintained while reducing the memory and calculation requirements. It therefore speeds up inference without significantly affecting the accuracy of the model. Listing 4.3 shows an example of Python code applying floating-point quantization (from fioat32 to fioati6) to a simple model with two linear layers. To demonstrate the effect of float quantization, we display a subset of the weights before and after quantization. Note that the instruction responsible for float quantization is "*model = model.to(torch.floati6)*".

Listing 4.3 - Floating point quantification

```
import torch
import torch.nn as nn

# Définition d'un modèle simple pour l'exemple
class SimpleModel(nn.Module):
    def __init__(self):
        super(SimpleModel, self).__init__()
        self.layer1 = nn.Linear(10, 5)
        self.layer2 = nn.Linear(5, 2)

    def forward(self, x):
        x = torch.relu(self.layer1(x))
        x = self.layer2(x)
        return x

# Création d'un modèle
model = SimpleModel()

# Sélection d'une couche spécifique pour l'exemple, ici layer1
selected_layer_weights_before = model.layer1.weight.data.clone()

# Afficher les valeurs de poids avant la conversion
print("Valeurs de poids avant la conversion (float32) :")
print(selected_layer_weights_before)

# Conversion du modèle en float16
model = model.to(torch.float16)

# Extraire les valeurs de poids après la conversion pour la même couche
selected_layer_weights_after = model.layer1.weight.data

# Afficher les valeurs de poids après la conversion
print("\nValeurs de poids après la conversion (float16) :")
print(selected_layer_weights_after)
```

4.2.5.3 Binary and ternary quantification

In these types of quantization, the representative values of the weights and/or activations of the neural network are quantized to just two values (binary quantization): +i and-1; or three values (ternary quantization): -1,*0* and +1. Listing 4.4 shows a Python example that illustrates binary quantization. This example applies binary quantisation to the weights of a model composed of a single linear layer. To do this, a "*BinarizeFunction*" class has been developed. Elie uses "*torch.autograd.Function*" to define a binary quantization function with a straight-through estimator (STE) for backpropagation. The forward method signs each weight value to convert it to -1 or +1. The backward method allows the gradient to be passed through the sign function during backpropagation, which is essential since the sign function is not differentiable at zero. Binary quantization is then used by the *BinarizedLinear* layer.

Listing 4.4 - Binary quantification

```
import torch
import torch.nn as nn
import torch.nn.functional as F

class BinarizeFunction(torch.autograd.Function):
    @staticmethod
    def forward(ctx, input):
        return input.sign()  # Retourne -1 ou 1 selon le signe de l'input

    @staticmethod
    def backward(ctx, grad_output):
        return grad_output  # Straight-through estimator

class BinarizedLinear(nn.Module):
    def __init__(self, input_features, output_features):
        super(BinarizedLinear, self).__init__()
        self.weight = nn.Parameter(torch.randn(output_features,
            input_features))
        self.bias = nn.Parameter(torch.randn(output_features))

    def forward(self, x):
        binarized_weight = BinarizeFunction.apply(self.weight)
        return F.linear(x, binarized_weight, self.bias)

# Initialisation du modèle
model = BinarizedLinear(input_features=10, output_features=2)

# Sauvegarde des poids originaux pour comparaison
original_weights = model.weight.data.clone()

print("Poids avant la quantification binaire :")
print(original_weights)

# Passage d'un exemple à travers le modèle pour appliquer la binarisation
input = torch.randn(1, 10)
model(input)

# Affichage des poids après la binarisation
print("\nPoids après la quantification binaire (appliquée durant le
    forward pass) :")
print(model.weight.data)

# Affichage des poids binarisés
# Note : La binarisation est appliquée durant le forward pass, donc les
    poids du modèle restent inchangés.
# Pour voir l'effet de la binarisation, on doit capturer et afficher les
    poids binarisés dans le forward.
binarized_weights = BinarizeFunction.apply(model.weight)
print("\nPoids binarisés explicitement :")
print(binarized_weights)
```

It should be noted that there are other types of quantisation, such as symmetrical quantisation and asymmetrical quantisation. Symmetric quantisation consists of maintaining symmetry (on either side of o) in the representation of weights. Asymmetric quantisation, on the other hand, represents weights in a wider range of positive values.

4.2.54 Quantification after training

Post-Training Quantization (PTQ) is generally applied to the weights obtained after training a neural network. The model is then trained and the quantification technique is applied to the resulting weights. This method can also be applied to activations. In this case, the model is initially trained with fairly precise activations. The quantification method is then applied. The post-training quantification steps are illustrated in Figure 4.3.

FIGURE 4.3 - Illustration of the steps involved in post-calibration quantification

Listing 4.5 shows pseudo Python code for post-training quantization. The first thing to do is to load a pre-trained model and apply the quantisation to this model. The data must of course be loaded.

Listing 4.5 - Post-entramming quantification

```
import torch
import torchvision.models as models

# Chargez un modèle pré-entraîné
model = models.resnet18(pretrained=True)
model.eval()

# Spécifiez la configuration de quantification
model.qconfig = torch.quantization.get_default_qconfig('fbgemm')

# Préparez le modèle pour la quantification
torch.quantization.prepare(model, inplace=True)

# Insérez ici votre logique pour passer les données à travers le modèle,
    ce qui est nécessaire pour
# le calibrage. Par exemple, utiliser un sous-ensemble de votre ensemble
    de validation.
# for data, target in data_loader:
#     model(data)

# Convertissez le modèle en modèle quantifié
torch.quantization.convert(model, inplace=True)

# Sauvegardez le modèle quantifié
torch.save(model.state_dict(), 'modele_quantifie.pth')

print("Le modèle a été quantifié et sauvé.")
```

Quantization can also be applied to each layer of the neural network. In general, the library can do this transparently. However, it is possible to see the loop explicitly if you use the tensorflow library (see the python code shown in listing 4.6).

Listing 4.6 - Quantification applied for each layer

Listing 4.6 – Quantification appliquée pour chaque couche

```
# Quantize weights
for layer in model.layers:
        if isinstance(layer, Dense):
                layer.kernel = quantize(layer.kernel)
                layer.bias = quantize(layer.bias)
```

Listing 4.7 illustrates the quantification of activations, using the tensorflow library. This quantification is applied to each layer of the neural network. It involves converting the original floating-point representations of the activations into a fixed-point representation. This can be achieved by rounding the activations to the nearest integer or by using a scaling factor to map the floating-point values to a smaller range of integer values.

Listing 4.7 - Quantification of activations (applied for each layer)

Listing 4.7 – Quantification des activations (appliquée pour chaque couche)

```
for i, layer in enumerate(model.layers):
        if isinstance(layer, Activation):
                model.layers[i] = Activation(quantize_activation)
```

It should be noted that the choice of quantification technique applied to activations depends very much on the activation function used to calculate them. For example, activations generated by the ReLU function will generally have to be processed using an asymmetric quantification approach in order to handle negative values.

This quantification technique (i.e., Post-Training Quantization) is easy to implement and can concern activations or weights, or both at the same time (i.e., hybrid quantification). On the other hand, post-training quantification can lead to a loss of precision and performance. This is because the quantisation is applied after training, so the model fails to take account of these reductions during training. This problem is avoided by the "quantification during training" method. This method is detailed in the following.

4"2.5"5 Quantification during training

This type of quantisation is called Quantization Aware Training (QAT). It involves applying the quantification to the initial weights. In this way, the learning phase remains aware of the quantification and the model will be learned on weights that have already been quantified. Figure 4.4 illustrates the different phases of the quantisation methodology during training.

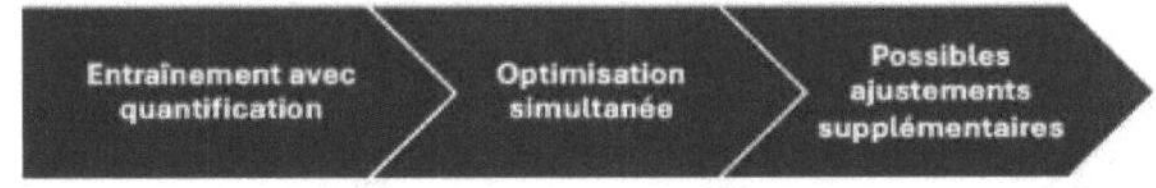

FIGURE 4.4 - Illustration of the quantification stages during training

To train the model with QAT in pytorch, we need to follow three steps. Firstly, we need to configure the model with QAT. Next, we need to train the model, taking into account the weights that have already been quantified. Finally, we convert the model to ensure quantified inference. The pseudo-code in listing 4.8 illustrates these different steps.

Listing 4.8 - Quantification of activations (applied for each layer)

Listing 4.8 – Quantification des activations (appliquée pour chaque couche)

```
# Importer les modules nécessaires
import torch
from torch.quantization import get_default_qat_qconfig, prepare_qat, convert

# Étape 1: Configurer le modèle pour QAT
model.qconfig = get_default_qat_qconfig('fbgemm') # Utiliser 'fbgemm' pour les serveurs ou 'qnnpack' pour les appareils mobiles
prepare_qat(model, inplace=True)

# Étape 2: Entraîner le modèle
# Assurez-vous que le modèle est en mode entraînement
model.train()
# Boucle d'entraînement standard ici
# optimizer.zero_grad()
# loss.backward()
# optimizer.step()

# Étape 3: Finaliser la quantification
# Après l'entraînement, passer le modèle en mode évaluation
model.eval()
# Convertir le modèle pour une inférence quantifiée
convert(model, inplace=True)

# Le modèle est maintenant prêt pour l'inférence quantifiée
```

4.3 Pruning

This section presents pruning and details its methods and strategies.

4.3.1 Definition of pruning

Pruning is a neural network optimisation technique. Pruning is used to eliminate weights that make a small contribution to prediction. Figure 4.5 illustrates the pruning process.

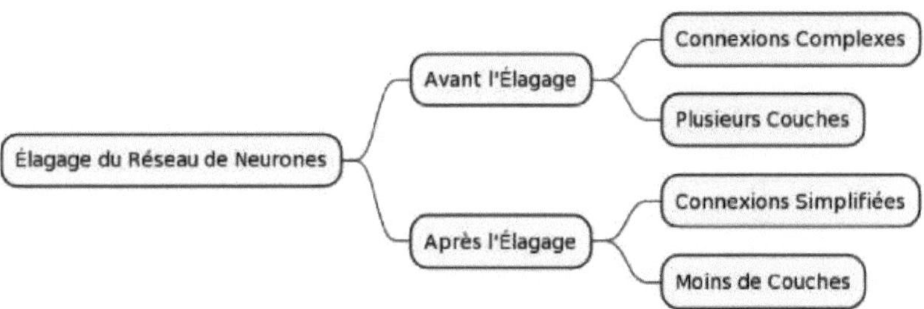

FIGURE 4.5 - Pruning process

Thus, pruning makes it possible to obtain a sparse model and consequently to reduce the size of the model without significantly affecting its performance. This reduction speeds up inference and helps to reduce energy consumption. Thus, pruning allows us to generate lightweight and efficient neural networks suitable for deployment on embedded systems. Figure 4.6 shows two neural networks before (i.e., dense network) and after pruning (i.e., sparse network).

In some cases, pruning makes it possible to get round the problem of overlearning, while eliminating superfluous connections. This will ensure a certain degree of generalisation, leading to better processing of the new data.

4.3.2 Pruning methods

There are various pruning methods, generally depending on the pruning criterion and the strategy applied. This book is limited to presenting a few pruning methodologies.

4.3.2.1 Random pruning

This method is not based on any criteria for removing weights. EUe simply does it in a random way. This makes its results unreliable. This method is generally used as a baseline to evaluate other pruning methodologies. The code in Listing 4.9 illustrates the random pruning method applied to a neural network with a rate of 30%.

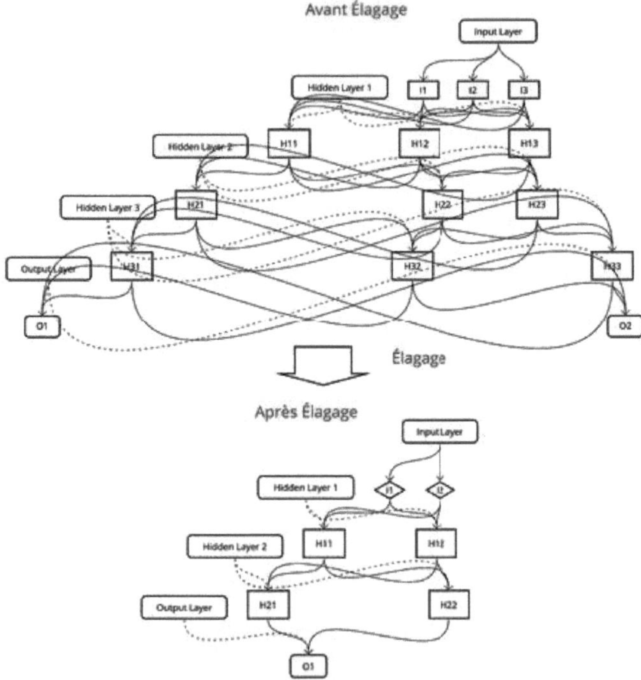

FIGURE 4.6 - Application of pruning to a neural network

Listing 4.9 – Élagage aléatoire de 30%

```python
import torch
import torch.nn.utils.prune as prune
import torch.nn as nn
class SimpleNet(nn.Module):
    def __init__(self):
        super(SimpleNet, self).__init__()
        self.fc1 = nn.Linear(784, 128)
        self.fc2 = nn.Linear(128, 64)
        self.fc3 = nn.Linear(64, 10)

    def forward(self, x):
        x = torch.relu(self.fc1(x))
        x = torch.relu(self.fc2(x))
        x = self.fc3(x)
        return x

model = SimpleNet()
# Élaguer 30% des connexions dans la première couche linéaire de manière
    aléatoire
prune.random_unstructured(model.fc1, name='weight', amount=0.3)
print("Poids après élagage:")
print(model.fc1.weight)

print("\nMasque de poids après élagage:")
print(model.fc1.weight_mask)
```

As shown in listing 4.9, we start by defining the model. Next, we randomly prune 30% of the connections in the first layer, using the *prune.random_unstructured* function. Finally, we display the weight values before and after pruning (see Figure 4.7). Note that weights whose values are 0 (after pruning) represent deleted weights.

```
Poids après élagage:
tensor([[ 0.0098,  0.0315,  0.0000,  ...,  0.0208, -0.0324,  0.0000],
        [ 0.0316,  0.0000, -0.0000,  ...,  0.0034,  0.0227,  0.0022],
        [ 0.0093, -0.0171, -0.0000,  ...,  0.0000,  0.0000,  0.0208],
        ...,
        [ 0.0000,  0.0218, -0.0161,  ..., -0.0000,  0.0000,  0.0157],
        [ 0.0201, -0.0048,  0.0000,  ...,  0.0059,  0.0225,  0.0000],
        [-0.0184, -0.0000,  0.0170,  ..., -0.0000,  0.0000, -0.0000]],
       grad_fn=<MulBackward0>)

Masque de poids après élagage:
tensor([[1., 1., 0.,  ..., 1., 1., 0.],
        [1., 0., 0.,  ..., 1., 1., 1.],
        [1., 1., 0.,  ..., 0., 0., 1.],
        ...,
        [0., 1., 1.,  ..., 0., 0., 1.],
        [1., 1., 0.,  ..., 1., 1., 0.],
        [1., 0., 1.,  ..., 0., 0., 0.]])
```

FIGURE 4.7 - Results of random pruning

4.3.2.2 Pruning based on magnitude

This method is based on the absolute values of the weights. Elie eliminates the weights with the lowest absolute values. This method considers that these weights do not contribute much to the decision. The code in listing4.10 illustrates the method of pruning based on magnitude, applied to the first layer of a neural network, with a rate of 30%.

Listing 4.10 - Pruning based on magnitude

Listing 4.10 – Élagage basé sur la magnitude

```python
import torch
import torch.nn as nn
import torch.nn.utils.prune as prune
class SimpleNet(nn.Module):
    def __init__(self):
        super(SimpleNet, self).__init__()
        self.fc1 = nn.Linear(784, 128)
        self.fc2 = nn.Linear(128, 64)
        self.fc3 = nn.Linear(64, 10)

    def forward(self, x):
        x = torch.relu(self.fc1(x))
        x = torch.relu(self.fc2(x))
        x = self.fc3(x)
        return x

model = SimpleNet()
# Élaguer 30% des poids de la première couche linéaire en fonction de
    leur magnitude
prune.l1_unstructured(model.fc1, name='weight', amount=0.3)
print("Poids après élagage :")
print(model.fc1.weight)

print("\nMasque de poids après élagage :")
print(model.fc1._forward_pre_hooks)
```

As shown in listing 4.9, we start by defining the model. Next, we perform pruning based on the magnitude of 30% of the connections in the first layer, using the *prune.l1_unstructured* function. Finally, we display the values of the weights after pruning (see Figure 4.8). Note that weights whose values are 0 (after pruning) represent deleted weights.

```
Poids après élagage :
tensor([[-0.0339,  0.0000,  0.0248,  ...,  0.0000,  0.0118, -0.0000],
        [ 0.0150, -0.0278,  0.0267,  ..., -0.0000,  0.0219, -0.0299],
        [ 0.0000,  0.0180,  0.0187,  ...,  0.0257, -0.0263, -0.0000],
        ...,
        [-0.0119, -0.0000,  0.0265,  ...,  0.0169, -0.0262,  0.0115],
        [-0.0000,  0.0135, -0.0267,  ..., -0.0182,  0.0000, -0.0322],
        [-0.0000, -0.0328,  0.0202,  ...,  0.0222, -0.0000, -0.0257]],
       grad_fn=<MulBackward0>)

Masque de poids après élagage :
OrderedDict([(1, <torch.nn.utils.prune.L1Unstructured object at 0x7e89ab1a2b00>)])
```

FIGURE 4.8 - Pruning results based on magnitude

4.3.2.3 Gradient-based pruning

This method consists of eliminating weights with a low gradient. In fact, it considers that these weights (i.e. those with low gradients) do not allow the loss function to be improved and consequently have a reduced and fairly low impact on the model's performance. The code in listing4.11 illustrates the gradient-based pruning process in a fairly simplistic way. First, we define and initialise the model. In this example, we use fictitious data. Next, we eliminate weights with a gradient below a certain threshold. This code is very simplistic and cannot really be applied in practice. The threshold must be selected very carefully. It is also important to restart the learning process to compensate for the loss of precision due to pruning.

Listing 4.11 - Gradient-based pruning

Listing 4.11 – Élagage basé sur la gradient

```
import torch
import torch.nn as nn
import torch.optim as optim

# Définir un modèle simple
class SimpleNet(nn.Module):
    def __init__(self):
        super(SimpleNet, self).__init__()
        self.fc = nn.Linear(10, 2)

    def forward(self, x):
        return self.fc(x)

# Initialiser le modèle, l'optimiseur et la fonction de perte
model = SimpleNet()
optimizer = optim.SGD(model.parameters(), lr=0.01)
criterion = nn.CrossEntropyLoss()

# Données fictives
inputs = torch.randn(5, 10)
targets = torch.randint(0, 2, (5,))
# Passe avant
outputs = model(inputs)
loss = criterion(outputs, targets)

# Zéro tous les gradients existants
optimizer.zero_grad()

# Rétropropagation
loss.backward()
# Obtenir les gradients absolus de la couche
gradients = torch.abs(model.fc.weight.grad)

# Calculer le seuil pour les 50% de gradients les plus faibles
threshold = torch.quantile(gradients, 0.5)

# Créer un masque où les gradients sont supérieurs au seuil
mask = gradients > threshold

# Appliquer le masque: mettre les poids sélectionnés à 0 (élagage)
with torch.no_grad():  # Assurez-vous de ne pas calculer de gradient ici
    model.fc.weight.data[mask.logical_not()] = 0.0
```

These pruning methods can be applied using a variety of strategies. This book details some of these strategies in section 4.3.3.

4.3.3 Pruning strategies

As pruning strategies, we detail in this book single pruning, iterative pruning and progressive pruning.

4.33'1 One-off pruning

Single pruning, also known as static pruning or one-step pruning, involves applying a pruning method only once to reduce the complexity of a neural network. Figure 4.9 illustrates the one-step pruning strategy. The first step is to train the model until optimal performance is achieved. Once the model is suitably learned, we set the pruning criterion(s) and hence the pruning methodology. This will be applied to our model to produce a sparse, less complex model whose inference is fairly straightforward. It is optional to re-train the model to take into account new weights (i.e. trimmed weights) and therefore improve the model's performance.

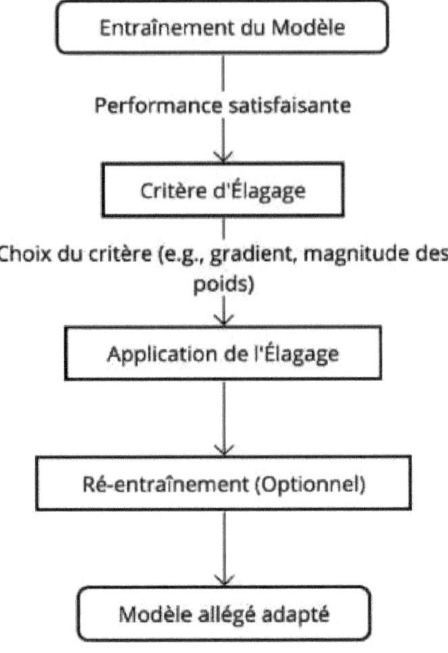

FIGURE 4.9 - Single pruning strategy

It should be noted that the single pruning strategy is fairly simple and quick. On the other hand, it is less flexible, since it does not include other iterations that allow for finer adjustment, taking into account the new weight values after trimming. As a result, one-off trimming can result in a significant loss of performance.

433'2 Iterative pruning

Unlike single pruning, iterative pruning goes through a number of pruning cycles to obtain a fairly effective separate model. Once the model has been properly tuned and satisfactory performance has been achieved, the second step is to apply pruning. This involves removing a fraction of the weights. This pruning step is followed by a training phase to adjust the remaining weights. This learning phase is repeated several times until a balanced model is found that provides a good compromise between efficiency and performance (see Figure 4.10).

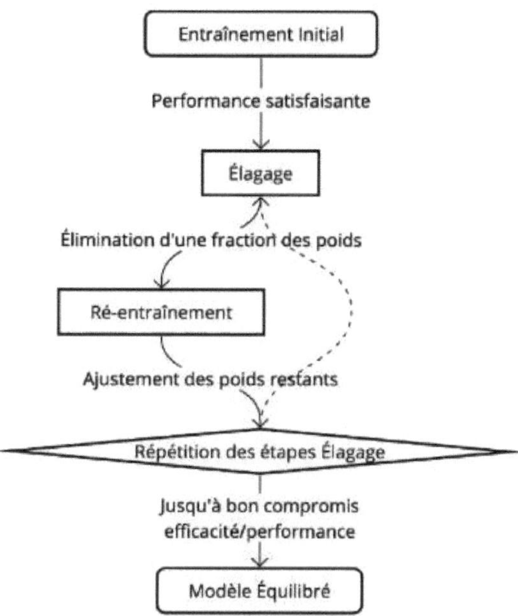

FIGURE 4.10 - Iterative pruning strategy

It is clear that iterative pruning is better than single pruning in terms of performance. In fact, the different pruning cycles ensure a better-learned model that is especially aware of elongated weights. However, this process is quite slow and complex, requiring particular attention to the planning of the different pruning cycles. Listing 4.12 illustrates the iterative pruning strategy applied to a deep learning model learned from the MNIST database. The learned model undergoes an iterative pruning strategy using the *iterative_pruning_and_retraining* function. This function allows several pruning cycles to be carried out. Each cycle is followed by a re-training phase on our model (i.e. the model initially learned from the MNIST database). Note that the number of iterations / cycles and the pruning rate must be adjusted according to the model and the training data.

Listing 4.12 - Iterative pruning

Listing 4.12 – Élagage itératif

```
import torch
import torch.nn as nn
import torch.optim as optim
import torch.nn.utils.prune as prune
from torchvision import datasets, transforms
from torch.utils.data import DataLoader

class SimpleNet(nn.Module):
    def __init__(self):
```

```
        super(SimpleNet, self).__init__()
        self.fc1 = nn.Linear(784, 128)  # 784 pour MNIST
        self.fc2 = nn.Linear(128, 10)

    def forward(self, x):
        x = torch.relu(self.fc1(x.view(-1, 784)))  # Aplatir l'image
            MNIST
        x = self.fc2(x)
        return x
transform = transforms.Compose([transforms.ToTensor(),
    transforms.Normalize((0.5,), (0.5,))])

train_dataset = datasets.MNIST(root='./data', train=True, download=True,
    transform=transform)
train_loader = DataLoader(train_dataset, batch_size=32, shuffle=True)

test_dataset = datasets.MNIST(root='./data', train=False, download=True,
    transform=transform)
test_loader = DataLoader(test_dataset, batch_size=1000, shuffle=False)
def train(model, device, train_loader, optimizer, epoch):
    model.train()
    for batch_idx, (data, target) in enumerate(train_loader):
        data, target = data.to(device), target.to(device)
        optimizer.zero_grad()
        output = model(data)
        loss = nn.CrossEntropyLoss()(output, target)
        loss.backward()
        optimizer.step()

device = torch.device("cuda" if torch.cuda.is_available() else "cpu")
model = SimpleNet().to(device)
optimizer = optim.SGD(model.parameters(), lr=0.01, momentum=0.5)
for epoch in range(1, 5):
    train(model, device, train_loader, optimizer, epoch)
def iterative_pruning_and_retraining(model, device, train_loader,
    optimizer, num_cycles=3, pruning_rate=0.2):
    for cycle in range(num_cycles):
        # Élagage
        parameters_to_prune = (
            (model.fc1, 'weight'),
        )
        prune.global_unstructured(parameters_to_prune,
            pruning_method=prune.L1Unstructured, amount=pruning_rate)

        # Ré-entraînement
        for epoch in range(1, 5):
            train(model, device, train_loader, optimizer, epoch)

        print(f"Cycle {cycle + 1}/{num_cycles} completed.")

iterative_pruning_and_retraining(model, device, train_loader, optimizer)
```

43'3'3 Progressive pruning

Progressive pruning is very similar to iterative pruning, except that it involves a gradual increase in the rate of pruning. This gradual increase in the rate of pruning ensures gradual conscious learning of pruning, resulting in sparse but effective and efficient neural networks. Figure 4.11 illustrates the gradual pruning process. First, we initialise the model. Then we prune at a low rate. The new weights (i.e., elagues) generated are then re-entered. In this way, this first training cycle is aware of the first pruning cycle, as in iterative pruning. This step is repeated while gradually increasing the rate of pruning. Once the desired criteria have been reached, the pruning process stops and we obtain an optimised model.

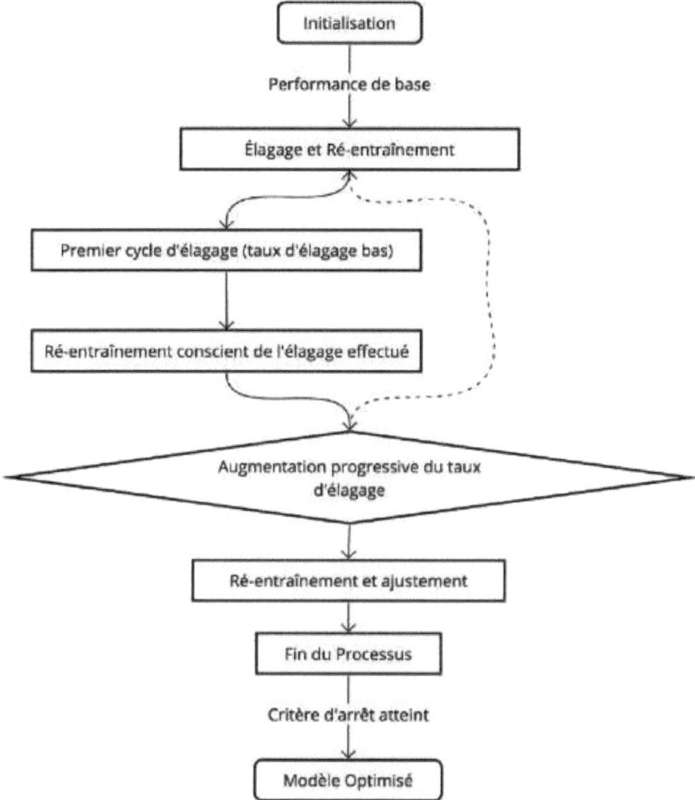

FIGURE 4.11 - Progressive pruning strategy

It should be noted that the advantages of progressive pruning lie in the fact that it ensures fine optimisation of the model by gradually increasing the pruning rate. On the other hand, determining the pruning rate can be difficult. Also, the implementation of this progressive process is complex.

The example in listing 4.13 illustrates the progressive pruning strategy on the same model learned from the MNIST database (see lines 1 - 37 in listing 4.12). Thus, this listing only shows the *progressive_pruning* function responsible for progressive pruning and its application to the model. This function begins by (1) setting a reduced pruning rate (=1%), (2) pruning the model and training it and (3) gradually increasing this pruning rate (*initial_pruning_rate* using the *pruning_rote_decoy* parameter (=0.2) (see line 23 of listing 4.13).

Listing 4.13 - Progressive pruning

Listing 4.13 – Élagage progressif

```
def progressive_pruning(model, device, train_loader, epochs_per_stage,
    initial_pruning_rate=0.1, pruning_rate_decay=0.2, num_stages=5):
    optimizer = optim.SGD(model.parameters(), lr=0.01, momentum=0.5)
    pruning_rate = initial_pruning_rate

    for stage in range(num_stages):
        # Définir les paramètres à élaguer
        parameters_to_prune = [(model.fc1, 'weight')]

        # Élagage global non structuré
        prune.global_unstructured(
            parameters=parameters_to_prune,
            pruning_method=prune.L1Unstructured,
            amount=pruning_rate,
        )

        # Ré-entraînement
        for epoch in range(1, epochs_per_stage + 1):
            train(model, device, train_loader, optimizer, epoch)

        print(f"Fin du stage {stage + 1}, taux d'élagage:
           {pruning_rate*100:.2f}%")

        # Augmenter le taux d'élagage pour le prochain cycle
        pruning_rate += pruning_rate_decay * pruning_rate

device = torch.device("cuda" if torch.cuda.is_available() else "cpu")
model = SimpleNet().to(device)
progressive_pruning(model, device, train_loader, epochs_per_stage=5,
    num_stages=3)
)
```

At this stage, it is important to note that the code examples presented in this chapter are for pedagogical purposes and are essentially used to explain the different concepts of quantisation and pruning. However, nowadays there are more sophisticated tools and libraries that allow the compression and optimisation of deep learning models in an easier way. These tools and libraries are detailed in section 4.4.

4.4 Tools used to compress DL models

There are a number of advanced tools and libraries that can be used to optimise deep learning models by applying pruning and quantification techniques.

quantification techniques. These include (1) the TensorFlow model optimisation toolkit and (2) NVIDIA TensorRT. This book gives details of these two tools.

4.4.1 The "TensorFlow" model optimisation toolkit

The "TensorFlow" model optimisation toolkit[1] is a toolkit for optimising Machine Learning and Deep Learning models, so that they can be deployed on mobile devices and resource-constrained equipment. This toolkit includes:

— An API for Integer Post-Training Quantization.

— An API for quantification during training (i.e. Quantization Aware Training)

— A PLC for pruning

— etc.

The models processed by these APIs must then be converted using Tensorflow Lite (TFLite[1 2]), so that they can be deployed on the corresponding hardware. TFLite is a tool for deploying and executing deep learning models on computers and equipment with limited resources.

4.4.2 NVIDIA TensorRT

NVIDIA TensorRT[3] is an SDK that includes an inference optimizer. It uses the quantization technique to optimize deep learning models. In particular, NVIDIA TensorRT uses integer and float quantization and applies it during training (QAT) and after training (PTQ), to optimize deep learning models and run them on resource-limited hardware.

4.5 Conclusion

This chapter has discussed two key techniques used to optimise deep learning models: quantification and pruning. The presentation of these techniques has been followed by various examples illustrating them. These examples can be run on Google Colab. The next chapter details another technique based on knowledge transfer, called Knowledge Distillation.

---

1 https ://www.tensorflow.org/model_optimization
2 https://www.tensorflow.org/lite
3 https ://developer.nvidia.com/tensorrt

Chapter 5

Distilling knowledge

5.1 Introduction

This chapter presents the knowledge distillation technique. This technique enables knowledge to be transferred from a large, high-performance deep learning model, known as a teacher, to a light, low-performance deep learning model, known as a student. The rest of the chapter is composed of seven sections. The first gives a general introduction to the knowledge distillation technique. The second section focuses on knowledge types. Next, we present the knowledge distillation methodology and knowledge types. We end this chapter with a practical implementation and a conclusion.

5.2 Distilling knowledge

The concept of knowledge distillation dates back to the 1980s. This concept was then formalised by Hinton and his co-authors, in 2015. Since then, this concept has evolved significantly and has been widely used in the field of deep automatic learning and embedded systems. Indeed, the knowledge distillation technique is very useful in the field of embedded systems. Indeed, the student model can be initially designed to be deployed on a dedicated hardware platform, thus satisfying all the constraints associated with it. The performance of this model will subsequently be improved, by learning from the knowledge transferred by the teaching model (a high-performance model by design).

Thus, the knowledge distillation technique is based on two main actors: (i) the "teacher" model and (ii) the "student" model. The teacher model is a very complex and therefore efficient model. The student model is much less complex and therefore much less effective than the teacher model. Knowledge distillation involves transferring knowledge from the teacher model to the student model. In this way, the student model learns not only from the labels verite terrain but also from the experience of the teacher model. Done, the student model remains capable of mimicking the teacher model's performance, by incorporating a condensed version of its knowledge. This allows us to improve the performance of a lightweight model designed primarily to be deployed and executed on lightweight equipment with limited resources.

As illustrated in Figure 5.1, the knowledge distillation process begins by training the teacher model on the basis of field truth labels. This step generates a well-learned teacher model. The knowledge set of the teacher model is transferred to the student model. In this way, the student model learns from the field truth labels and the knowledge of the teacher model.

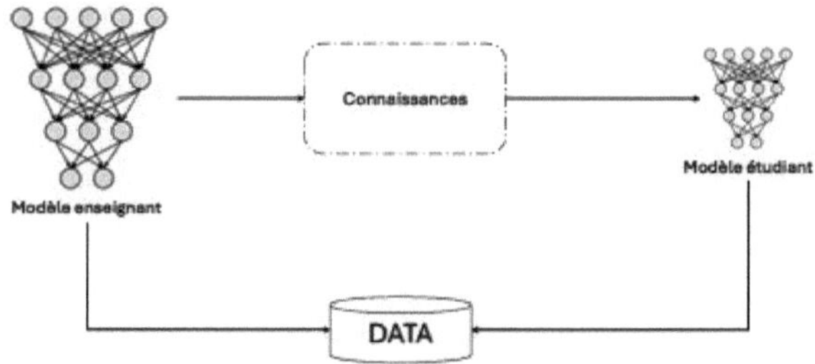

FIGURE 5.1 - Knowledge distillation

The knowledge distillation technique depends on the nature of the knowledge transferred from the teacher model to the student model. The types of knowledge are detailed in section 5.3.

5.3 Types of knowledge

There are various types of knowledge that can be transferred from a teacher model to a student model. This book details four types.

5.3.1 Type 1: Logits

The logits represent the outputs of the last layer of a neural network, just before the softmax function is applied to obtain the probabilities. Transferring these logits from the teacher model to the student model makes it possible to transmit not only the final predictions but also the relative confidence of the teacher model in these predictions. In this way, the student model is able to learn fine nuances in the decisions made by the teacher model and, as a result, will be able to generalise to new data.

5.3.2 Type 2: Intermediate characteristics

Intermediate characteristics, also known as internal representations or hidden layer activations, are the representations learned at different layers of the teaching neural networks. They reflect the internal processing of the input data and capture abstract information. By transferring these characteristics from the teacher model to the student model, the latter (i.e. the student model) benefits from the expertise and deep understanding of the data acquired by the teacher model. This speeds up the learning process and improves the student model's ability to generalise.

5.3.3 Type 3: Relational knowledge

Relational knowledge in the context of knowledge distillation refers to information about the relationships and dynamics between different inputs, classes, or characteristics within the teacher model. Contrastive Representation Distillation (CRD) is an advanced technique that aims to transfer this relational knowledge from the teacher model to the student model. This approach helps the student model to develop a deeper understanding of the data, focusing on relationships rather than isolated features. This can be particularly useful in complex tasks where relationships between data are crucial.

5.3.4 Type 4: Attention knowledge and decision dynamics

Around 2014 and 2015, the attention mechanism emerged in the context of natural language processing. This mechanism allows machine learning models to focus on the most relevant parts of the input data when making a decision. In the context of natural language processing (NLP), the model can give more attention (i.e. importance) to certain words, which can generally encompass the meaning of the sentence.

The transfer of attentional knowledge consists of passing on to the student model the parts of the data considered important for the decision (e.g. areas of an image considered important by the teacher model for identifying an object). In this way, the student model can "see" and "understand" which parts of the data have been considered important by the teacher model.

In addition to transferring attentional knowledge, it is possible for the teacher model to transfer decision dynamics to the student model. This involves transferring processing paths that the teacher model uses to arrive at its predictions. This allows the student model to imitate the teacher model's decision-making behaviour.

There are various methods of transferring knowledge, depending on the type of knowledge being transferred. This book details only the logit transfer methodology in the context of knowledge distillation. This method is detailed in section 5.4.

5.4 Knowledge distillation methodology

All knowledge distillation methods share the same first step. They all start by training the teacher model. In the case where the knowledge to be transferred is logits, these are used to determine the decisions for each example of data, using the trained teacher model. The logits represent the outputs of the model before the application of the softmax function, thus representing non-normalised scores for each class. The third step consists in (1) defining the student model which is necessarily smaller and less complex than the teacher model, (2) training the student model using a combination of the true class labels (i.e., ground truth labels) and the teacher model outputs, terminated using the logits. The training of the ground truth labels is done as usual using the traditional cross-entropy loss function expressed by formula 5.1.

(5.1) $$L_{S_c} = C(softmax(l_s), y)$$

Where C is the cross-entropy loss, and y represents the true label.

Learning from the logits of the teacher model is based on the *Kullback-Leibler* (KL) divergence loss function, expressed by formula 5.2.

(5.2) $$L_{KD} = \tau^2 KL(l_s, l_t)$$

Where τ is the temperature hyper-parameter, which is introduced to control the attenuation of the signal caused by the output of the teaching network.

$_s$ and$_t$ are the logits of the teacher and student models, respectively.

The output of each network can be expressed as $y_s = softmax(l_s/\tau)$ et $y_t = softmax(l_t/\tau)$.

Consequently, the student model will be entered using the loss function expressed by formula (5.3):

(5.3) $$L_{Student} = (1 - \lambda)L_{S_c} + \lambda L_{KD}$$

With λ is the second hyper-parameter used to balance the dassic loss function of the student model and the divergence loss function.

Figure 5.2 illustrates the knowledge distillation method in the case where the transferred knowledge is logit.

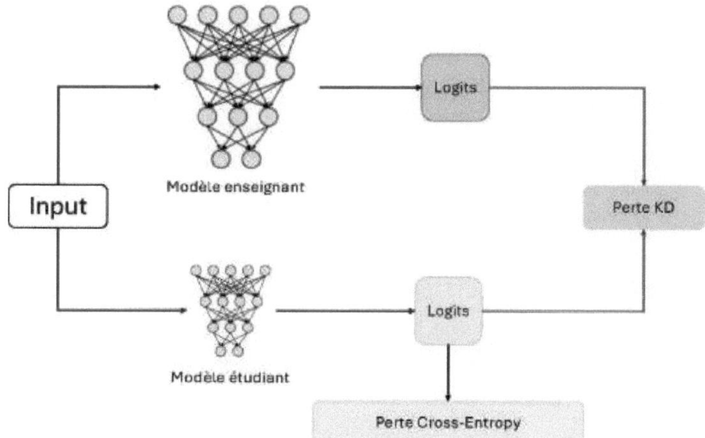

FIGURE 5.2 - Knowledge distillation

5.5 Types of knowledge distillation

There are several types/schemes of knowledge distillation. The best known is offline knowledge distillation. This is the type described in the previous sections. In addition to this type, there are other types such as online knowledge distillation and self-distillation. These types will be described in the following.

5.5.1 Offline knowledge distillation

Offline knowledge distillation represents the classic type of distillation. This is the type described earlier in this chapter. It involves training the teacher model offline. The knowledge from this model will then be transferred to the student model. This type of distillation is characterised by its simplicity of implementation. The distillation process is linear in the sense that the teacher model is trained, and then the student model is trained on the basis of the output from the teacher model. It is also possible to use the knowledge of the teacher model to train various student models. This saves computational resources. Also, offline knowledge distillation allows us to easily test several student models (architecture, model size), while using the same knowledge from the teacher model. However, the offline knowledge distillation technique has a few drawbacks. Firstly, this technique does not allow for simple and flexible updating of knowledge. In fact, once the knowledge of the teacher model has been determined, any update requires the whole process to be repeated from the beginning. This is very time-consuming. Also, there is a need for additional memory resources to store the outputs of the teacher model. Finally, offline knowledge distillation suffers from the problem of the gap between the capabilities of the student model and the teacher model. This gap will affect the performance of the student model, which will not be able to learn properly from the teacher model. The gap problem has been addressed by several researchers. Several solutions have been proposed in the literature.

5.5.2 Online knowledge distillation

Unlike offline knowledge distillation, online knowledge distillation does not require the teacher model to be fully trained in advance in order to begin the process of transferring knowledge to the student model. Figure 5.3 illustrates online knowledge distillation. The teacher and student models are trained simultaneously. In this way, all the knowledge of the teacher model is transferred in a progressive and iterative way to the student model.

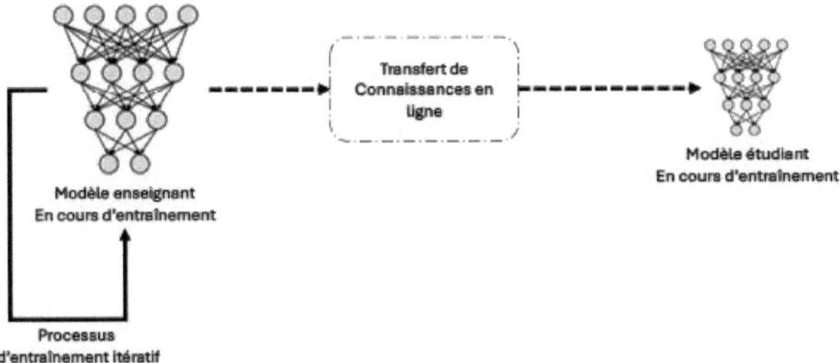

FIGURE 5.3 - Online knowledge distillation

Online distillation is therefore based on interactivity between the teacher and student models. This interactivity allows greater flexibility in the learning process, leading to a more generalised and more effective student model.

There are various approaches to online distillation, which have been widely proposed by researchers. In this chapter we mention the best-known approach, namely the mutual learning approach.

Mutual learning involves several student models and one teacher model in the learning process. These models

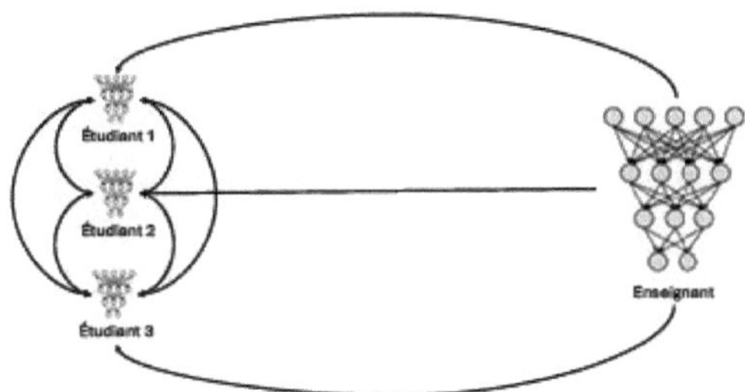

FIGURE 5.4 - Online knowledge distillation: Mutual learning approachStudents learn not only from the teacher model but also from each other (see Figure 5.4). In this way, mutual learning enables rich interaction between the student models as each benefits from the strengths of the others and consequently compensates for the weaknesses of the others through the distillation process.

5.5.3 Auto-distillation

Self-distillation is a special case of online knowledge distillation. It allows a model to learn from itself, iteratively and incrementally. As illustrated in Figure 5.5, the student model is first enframed on the true labels. It is then re-framed on a dataset enriched with its own predictions from the previous iteration. This helps to (1) gradually incorporate new knowledge, (2) refine the model's predictive capabilities and (3) reduce overlearning. In fact, the model is trained on a slightly altered version of the original data, which can help to diversify and generalise learning.

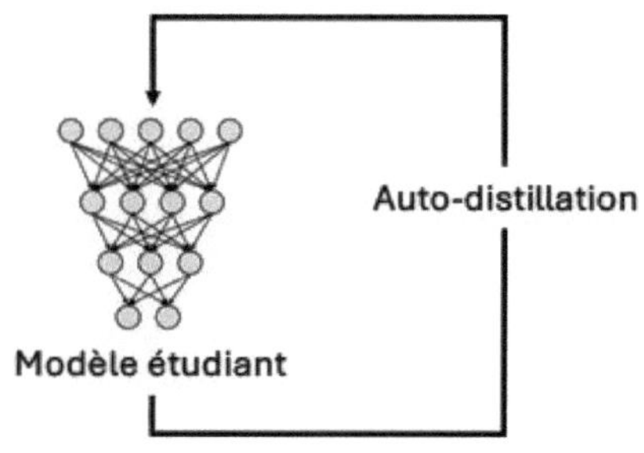

FIGURE 5.5 - Self-distillation

5.6 Practical implementation

This section gives a Python implementation of knowledge distillation, based on the use of the "*pytorch*" library. The first task is to (1) define a complex teacher model capable of classifying images from the CIFAR-10 database and (2) a simple student model capable of doing the same thing. The objective of this Python code is to compare (i) the performance of the student model when learned on true labels only and (ii) its performance when learned using a knowledge distillation method. Thus, our code begins by loading the necessary libraries (see listing 5.1).

Listing 5-1 ~ Step 1: Load the necessary libraries

Listing 5.1 – Étape 1 : Charger les librairies nécessaires

```
import torch
import torch.nn as nn
import torch.nn.functional as F
import torch.optim as optim
from torchvision import datasets, transforms

from torch.utils.data import DataLoader
from torchvision.models import resnet18  # Modèle pré-entrainé utilisé
    pour l'enseignant
```

Next, our code defines the teacher model, which is based on the pre-trained *"ResNet 18"* model (see listing 5.2).

Listing 5.2 - Step 2: Defining the teacher model

Listing 5.2 – Étape 2 : Définir le modèle enseignant

```
# Définir le modèle enseignant en utilisant le modèle pré-entrainé
    ResNet18
class TeacherModel(nn.Module):
    def __init__(self, pretrained=True, num_classes=10):
        super(TeacherModel, self).__init__()
        self.model = resnet18(pretrained=pretrained)
        self.model.fc = nn.Linear(self.model.fc.in_features, num_classes)

    def forward(self, x):
        return self.model(x)
```

The third step is to define the student model. This is a very simple model based on the use of a CNN (see listing 5.3).

Listing 5.3 - Step 3: Defining the student model

Listing 5.3 – Etape 3 : Définir le modèle étudiant

```
# Define the Student Model (simpler CNN)
class StudentModel(nn.Module):
    def __init__(self):
        super(StudentModel, self).__init__()
        self.conv1 = nn.Conv2d(3, 32, kernel_size=3, padding=1)
        self.conv2 = nn.Conv2d(32, 64, kernel_size=3, padding=1)
        self.fc1 = nn.Linear(64 * 8 * 8, 120)
        self.fc2 = nn.Linear(120, 10)

    def forward(self, x):
        x = F.max_pool2d(F.relu(self.conv1(x)), 2)
        x = F.max_pool2d(F.relu(self.conv2(x)), 2)
        x = x.view(-1, 64 * 8 * 8)
        x = F.relu(self.fc1(x))
        x = self.fc2(x)
        return x
```

The fourth step is to load the data from the CIFAR10 database (see listing 5.4). This database contains 60,000 coloured images (32*32), belonging to 10 classes .[1]

Listing 5.4 - Step 4: Loading the CIFAR 10 database

Listing 5.4 – Étape 4 : Chargement de la base de données CIFAR 10

```
# Load CIFAR-10 data
transform = transforms.Compose([
    transforms.ToTensor(),
    transforms.Normalize((0.5, 0.5, 0.5), (0.5, 0.5, 0.5))
])

train_dataset = datasets.CIFAR10(root='./data', train=True,
   download=True, transform=transform)
train_loader = DataLoader(train_dataset, batch_size=64, shuffle=True)

test_dataset = datasets.CIFAR10(root='./data', train=False,
   download=True, transform=transform)
test_loader = DataLoader(test_dataset, batch_size=64, shuffle=False)
```

Once the two models have been defined and the data loaded, we can proceed to initialise the data (see listing 5.5).

Listing 5.5 - Step 5: Loading the CIFAR-10 database

Listing 5.5 – Étape 5 : Chargement de la base de données CIFAR-10

```
# Initialiser les modèles
teacher_model = TeacherModel(pretrained=False)
student_model = StudentModel()
```

The sixth step is to define the drive parameters (see listing 5.6).

Listing 5.6 - Step 6: Definition of learning settings

Listing 5.6 – Étape 6 : Définition de settings de l'apprentissage

```
device = torch.device("cuda" if torch.cuda.is_available() else "cpu")
teacher_model.to(device)
student_model.to(device)
optimizer = optim.Adam(student_model.parameters(), lr=0.001)
```

We now define two learning functions. The first is used to train the student model based on true labels only (see listing 5.7).

Listing 5.7 - Step 7.1: Defining the learning function of the student model based on the true labels

```
def train_student_with_hard_labels(student_model, device, train_loader,
    optimizer, epoch):
    student_model.train()
    for batch_idx, (data, target) in enumerate(train_loader):
        data, target = data.to(device), target.to(device)
        optimizer.zero_grad()
        output = student_model(data)
        loss = F.cross_entropy(output, target)
        loss.backward()
        optimizer.step()
        if batch_idx % 100 == 0:
            print(f'Hard Labels Epoch: {epoch} [{batch_idx *
                len(data)}/{len(train_loader.dataset)} ({100. * batch_idx
                / len(train_loader):.0f}%)]\tLoss: {loss.item():.6f}')
```

The second is used to train the model using the knowledge distillation method. In this case, it is also necessary to define the loss function (i.e., distillation loss), as illustrated by Listing 5.8.

Listing 5.8 - Step 7.1: Defining the learning function of the student model <u>using the knowledge distillation methodology</u>

```
# Distillation de connaissances
def train_student(teacher_model, student_model, device, train_loader,
    optimizer, epoch, temperature=2.0, alpha=0.5):
    teacher_model.eval()
    student_model.train()
```

```
    for batch_idx, (data, target) in enumerate(train_loader):
        data, target = data.to(device), target.to(device)
        optimizer.zero_grad()
        teacher_output = teacher_model(data)
        student_output = student_model(data)
        loss = distillation_loss(student_output, teacher_output, target,
            temperature, alpha)
        loss.backward()
        optimizer.step()
        if batch_idx % 100 == 0:
            print(f'Train Epoch: {epoch} [{batch_idx *
                len(data)}/{len(train_loader.dataset)} ({100. * batch_idx
                / len(train_loader):.0f}%)]\tLoss: {loss.item():.6f}')

# Fonction perte
def distillation_loss(student_outputs, teacher_outputs, true_labels,
    temperature, alpha):
    soft_loss = nn.KLDivLoss()(F.log_softmax(student_outputs /
        temperature, dim=1), F.softmax(teacher_outputs / temperature,
        dim=1))
    hard_loss = F.cross_entropy(student_outputs, true_labels)
    return alpha * soft_loss + (1 - alpha) * hard_loss
```

Before starting to learn the student model, we need to define a function to evaluate the learning process. The code for this function is given in listing 5.9.

Listing 5-9 - Definition of the learning assessment function

Listing 5.9 – Définition de la fonction d'évaluation de l'apprentissage

```
# fonction de test permettant l'évaluation du modèle étudiant
def test(model, device, test_loader):
    model.eval()
    test_loss = 0
    correct = 0
    with torch.no_grad():
        for data, target in test_loader:
            data, target = data.to(device), target.to(device)
            output = model(data)
            test_loss += F.cross_entropy(output, target,
               reduction='sum').item()  # sum up batch loss
            pred = output.argmax(dim=1, keepdim=True)  # get the index
               of the max log-probability
            correct += pred.eq(target.view_as(pred)).sum().item()
    test_loss /= len(test_loader.dataset)
    print(f'\nTest set: Average loss: {test_loss:.4f}, Accuracy:
       {correct}/{len(test_loader.dataset)} ({100. * correct /
       len(test_loader.dataset):.0f}%)\n')
```

Once all the steps described above have been completed, we can start learning the student model. We begin by applying the first learning function, based on true labels only (see listing 5.10). After training, the model will be evaluated using the function in Listing 5.9.

Listing 5.10 - Step 8.1 : Learning and evaluation of the student model: Learning based on real labels

```
# Apprentissage du modèle étudiant en se basant sur les vrais labels

for epoch in range(1, 11):  # Let's train for 10 epochs
    print(f"Epoch {epoch}/10 - Training with Hard Labels")
    train_student_with_hard_labels(student_model, device, train_loader,
       optimizer, epoch)

# Évaluation du modèle étudiant
test(student_model, device, test_loader)
```

This code was run on Google Colab, using the T4 GPU. The results obtained showed that the accuracy of the model (i.e. accuracy) is 70%.

As shown in listing 5.11, step 8.2 consists of learning the student model, following the knowledge distillation methodology. Once the model is learned, we evaluate it. In this case, we notice that the model's performance has improved when we followed a knowledge distillation approach. In particular, accuracy improved by 2% to 72%.

Listing 5.11 - Step 8.2 : Learning and evaluating the student model: Knowledge distillation

Listing 5.11 – Étape 8.2 : Apprentissage et évaluation du modèle étudiant : Distillation de connaissances

```
# Apprentissage en suivant la distillation de connaissances
for epoch in range(1, 11):  # Let's train for 10 epochs
    print(f"Epoch {epoch}/10 - Training with Knowledge Distillation")
    train_student(teacher_model, student_model, device, train_loader,
       optimizer, epoch)


#Évaluation du modèle étudiant
test(student_model, device, test_loader)
```

5.7 Conclusion

This chapter has explored a current technique, namely knowledge distillation. This technique is used to transfer knowledge from a complex, high-performing teacher model to a simple, non-performing student model. Knowledge distillation helps to greatly improve the performance of the student model (i.e., the simple model), while retaining its simplicity. This will enable a good compromise to be found between performance and model size. This ensures that the model can be deployed effectively on resource-constrained hardware.

Chapter б

General conclusion

This book dealt with a topical subject, namely embedded machine learning. It began by discussing the key concepts related to this theme. Thus, the book included a chapter on machine learning, showing its theoretical foundations and explaining the learning process and its different phases. Chapter 3 was an opportunity to explore the world of the Internet of Things: a concept closely related to the main theme of this book.

Next, we set out to develop techniques for compressing, optimising and transferring the knowledge employed in the context of machine learning in order to reduce the gap between the performance required by deep learning models and the capabilities of connected objects. Reducing this gap will enable deep learning models to be deployed effectively on connected objects. This leads us to embedded machine learning.

Chapter да details the quantification technique and illustrated its application on deep learning models, through Python implementations. Also, this same chapter presented the pruning technique, while demonstrating its feasibility in the context of machine learning.

The fifth chapter was devoted to knowledge distillation: a new knowledge transfer paradigm between a complex, high-performance model (i.e., teacher) and a simple, low-performance model (i.e., student). This technique was also illustrated through a practical implementation based on the use of the pytorch library.

Bibliographic

[1] Geoffrey Hinton, Oriol Vinyals, Jeff Dean, et al. Distilling the knowledge in a neural network. In *NIPS Deep Learning and Representation Learning Workshop,* Montreal, Canada, 2015. Curran Associates, Inc.

[2] YingZhang, Tao Xiang, Timothy M Hospedales, and Huchuan Lu. Deep mutual learning. In *Proceedings of the IEEE Conference on Computer Vision and Pattern Recognition,* Salt Lake City, UT, USA, 2018. IEEE.

[3] YonglongTian, Dilip Krishnan, and Phillip Isola. Contrastive representation distillation. In *Proceedings of the International Conference on Learning Representations(ICLR),* Addis Ababa, Ethiopia, 2020.

[4] Salma Daoud, AfefMdhaffar, Mohamed Jmaiel,and Bernd Freisleben. Q-Rank: Reinforcement Learning for Recommending Algorithms to Predict Drug Sensitivity to Cancer Therapy. *IEEE Journal of Biomedical and Health Informatics,* 24(11), 2020.

[5] Jianping Gou, Baosheng Yu, Stephen J Maybank, and Dacheng Tao. Knowledge distillation: A survey. *International Journal of Computer Vision,* 129,2021.

[6] AbirAffes,AfefMdhaffar, ChahnezTriki, Mohamed Jmaiel,and Bernd Freisleben. Personalized attention-based EEG channel selection for epileptic seizure prediction. *Expert Systems with Applications,* 206, 2022.

[7] AfefMdhaffar, BechirZalila, Racem Moalla, Ayoub Kharrat, Omar Rebai, Mohamed Me- lek Hsairi, Ahmed Sallemi, Hsouna Kobbi, Amel Kolsi, Dorsaf Chatti, Mohamed Jmaiel, and Bernd Freisleben. A smart trap for counting olive moths based on the internet of thingsand deep learning. In *Proceedings of the 19th IEEE/ACS International Conference on Computer Systems and Applications (AICCSA)* ,Abu Dhabi, UAE, December2022. IEEE.

[8] Nurbiya Yadikar, Kurban Ubul, et al. A review of knowledge distillation in object detection. *IEEE Access,* 11,2023.

[9] Loth Souifi, AfefMdhaffar, Ismael Bouassida Rodriguez, Mohamed Jmaiel, and Bernd Freisleben. InsectDSOT : A Neural Network for Insect Detection in Olive Trees. In *15th International Conference on Agents and Artificial Intelligence, (ICAART),* Lisbon, Portugal, February 2023. SCITEPRESS.

[10]Emna Guermazi, Afef Mdhaffar, Mohamed Jmaiel, and Bernd Freisleben. LIDL4Oliv:A Lightweight Incremental Deep Learning Model for Classifying Olive Diseases in Images. In *16th International Conference on Agents and Artificial Intelligence, (ICAART),* Rome, Italy, February 2024. SCITEPRESS.

More
Books!

OMNIScriptum

Printed by Books on Demand GmbH, Norderstedt / Germany